Muse the Mule

by Dottie Raymer
illustrated by Jan Pyk

Core Decodable 68

McGraw Hill Education

Bothell, WA • Chicago, IL • Columbus, OH • New York, NY

MHEonline.com

Send all inquiries to:
McGraw-Hill Education
8787 Orion Place
Columbus, OH 43240

ISBN: 978-0-02-144337-6
MHID: 0-02-144337-8

Printed in Canada.

9 10 11 12 KOD 24

Muse is a cute mule.

Muse had a forest home.

Muse liked the forest.

But Muse liked music the most.

Hugo cut branches and traded them.
Muse had to lug the branches on his back.

Muse did not like branches on his back.
Muse did not budge.

At last, Hugo made music for Muse.

Muse did not like big branches on his back.
But Muse liked Hugo's music.